MW00682517

This book is a special gift

To:

_____

From:

_____

Date:

_____

Message:

_____

_____

365 Things that every Parent should know

Solly Ozrovech

Christian Art Gifts

Originally published by Christian Publishing Company under
the title *365 Dinge wat elke ouer moet weet* © 1996

This edition published by Christian Art Gifts
PO Box 1599, Vereeniging, 1930, South Africa

© 2000

Translated by Linda Beukes

Cover designed by Christian Art Gifts

Scripture quotations are taken from
the *Holy Bible*, King James Version

Printed in Singapore

ISBN 1-86852-655-0

00 01 02 03 04 05 06 07 08 09 - 10 9 8 7 6 5 4 3 2 1

365 Things that every Parent should know

Index

Foreword

Upbringing (1-78)

Love (79-93)

Religion (94-110)

Discipline (111-147)

School and achievements (148-171)

Communication (172-188)

Vacation, sport and leisure (189-225)

Money and material
possessions (226-242)

Adolescence (243-256)

Humour and laughter (257-265)

Marriage (266-272)

Television (273-279)

Emergency situations (280-285)

Food and meals (286-300)

General (301-365)

Foreword

One of the most difficult tasks on earth is being a good parent. In this top ranking job we all, to a greater or lesser extent, have success. We are deeply dependent on the mercy of God who grants us the wisdom and competence to fulfil this task. That is why the psalmist says: *Except the Lord build the house, they labour in vain that build it* (Ps. 127:1). In this great task we must help each other and pray for each other. Every parent will most probably be able to list 365 things we should do to raise our children in the correct way. In modesty and deep awareness of my own shortcomings as a parent, I offer this book to the reader. I do hope that something in this book may give you some food for thought and help you in your huge task of parenthood.

Soli Deo gloria!

~ Solly Ozrovech, Strand ~

UPBRINGING (1-78)

It is every child's birthright to be brought up by his parents. Scripture also requires that parents raise a child with knowledge and love of God, his parents and his neighbour. Putting your mind to this is not only an instruction from God, but also provides lifelong joy.

1

that you ought to avoid
labels. They are more
suited to cans and bottles.

2

that you cannot protect your children
against all dangers and problems.

3

that boys need a
father figure and girls
need a mother figure.

4

how to encourage
responsibility in your children.

5

that children need individual
treatment on a one-to-one
basis from their parents.

6

how to think of a convincing
answer to a difficult question.

7

that children should
learn that grown-ups can
also sometimes be wrong.

8

that no child arrives in this
world with an owner's manual.

Every parent should know ...

9

when to apologise to your child.

10

how to succeed in
parenthood, even if it
is only in one specific field.

11

that democracy does
not always work
within the family unit.

12

to knock before
entering a child's room.

13

the answer to every
question from a child.

14

what expectations to
scale down on with
regard to your child.

<u>15</u>

how to reward your children.

<u>16</u>

to discover the good in
your children rather than
constantly hammering
on their weaknesses.

<u>17</u>

not to constantly find fault
with your children and in the process
discourage them (cf. Col. 3:21).

<u>18</u>

that a home should be a
place of emotional safety.

<u>19</u>

not to compare your
children to one another.

<u>20</u>

which things motivate your children.

<u>21</u>

that children hear
everything that their parents say.

22

how to inspire your children to
make a difference in this world.

23

how to comfort a child
with a broken heart.

24

Even a child is known by
his doings, whether his
work be pure, and whether
it be right (Prov. 20:11).

25

that parents can only do
their best and the rest
should be left to God.

26:

that children will fall off swings
and out of trees – and will
make some bad decisions.

27

not to complain about
your child's loud music
when you have given
him a CD for his birthday.

28

that there are no such
things as perfect parents.

29

that you don't have to be a rocket
scientist to be a good parent.

30

that you know your
child better than
anyone else on earth.

31

that a child's behaviour
is a reflection of his
circumstances at home.

32

to praise your child at
least once every day.

33

how to defuse jealousy
between siblings.

<u>34</u>

that punctuality is a
very important virtue.

<u>35</u>

that character is built
through discovery and failure.

<u>36</u>

that it would require maturity
to avoid reprisal, but that it would
also create a sense of security.

37

that children in the house
should share in the house-
hold duties in order to feel
that they are part of the family.

38

that which is wonderful for
other children may not
necessarily be wonderful for yours.

39

that children should
have many more good
memories than bad ones.

40 ☆

who the parents of his
children's friends are.

41

the words of "Peter Piper picked
a pack of pickled peppers."

42

when to hold your children
responsible for their own acts.

43

that your children use your
attitude towards them
as a criterion to determine
their own personality and value.

44

to teach tolerance by example.

45

how to teach your child to handle
insults and compliments.

46

how to help your
child develop his
decision-making skills.

47

that even the best cricket
players are sometimes,
just like their parents,
caught leg before wicket.

48

that pets teach a
child responsibility.

<u>49</u>

how to teach your
children to ask questions.

<u>50</u>

that you are going to be
called the worst parents
in the world at least once.

<u>51</u>

that it is more difficult to say
"no" than giving in to pressure.

52

that children sometimes
enjoy seeing that parents
can also break the rules.

53

that spoiling a child
eventually turns him into a loser.

54

that you ought to encourage
your child in front of others.

Every parent should know ...

55

that it takes more or
less three weeks to learn
or unlearn a habit.

56

you ought to compliment
each and every hand-
made creation of your child.

57

that it is far more important to know
how to think than what to think.

Every parent should know ...

<u>58</u>

to discover ways to
respect your child's feelings.

<u>59</u>

how to teach your children
to look for the right answers.

<u>60</u>

how to build character.

61

how to understand the physical
and emotional stages that
every child goes through from
being a toddler to a teenager
and then to being a grown-up.

62

that encouragement is
like oxygen for the heart.

63

how to cultivate respect in your
children by respecting them.

64

how to be an example of integrity.

65

how to encourage
the acquisition of
knowledge by being
involved with your children.

66

how to pay attention to
what is really going
on in your child's heart.

Every parent should know ...

67

that you should teach your
children how to handle conflict.

68

that patience is a characteristic
that pays off immensely
for the rest of your life.

69

to enthusiastically celebrate
the slightest sign of
progress with your child.

~ 33 ~

70

that children should have
responsibilities in the house.

71

that children forget
quickly and easily.

72

that a child flourishes
when he is trusted.

73

that the problems a child
experiences may seem
insignificant, but could
be overwhelming to him.

74

that it is sometimes good
for men and boys to cry.

75

that children love winning,
especially against their parents.

76

that children might imitate
heroes, but that they are
really looking for role models.

<u>77</u>

that a night light has a
calming effect on a child.

<u>78</u>

that successful education
starts in the home.

LOVE (79-93)

*In the family love is imperative because it is
the factor that binds the family together and
prevents it from falling apart. The family is the
place where the child should experience the real
meaning of love and learn to apply it in his or
her life.*

<u>79</u>

when a child needs a hug desperately.

<u>80</u>

that love is a verb.

<u>81</u>

how to physically express your love.

<u>82</u>

how to say, "I love you!"
in twenty different ways.

83

that a friendly word is never forgotten.

84

that unconditional love is always risky.

85

that discipline must be followed by hugs and kisses.

86

that love provides a protective cover for your child.

87

never to hold back love
in order to punish your
child for his poor performance.

88

to show your love and
approval in spite of what is written
on your child's report card.

89

how to love unconditionally.

90

that God's love is perfect.

91

that criticism is always painful.

92

that children older than ten
don't want to be seen in public,
but that it doesn't necessarily mean
that it should be avoided altogether.

93

to put on a plaster even if
there isn't even a trace of blood.

RELIGION (94-110)

God sows the seeds of religion in every human heart. Parents have the privilege and the responsibility to nurture and cultivate these seeds in order for them to grow and develop fully and to yield an abundant harvest.

94

the just man walketh in his integrity: his children are blessed after him (Prov. 20:7).

95

that a child receives his religion together with his mother's milk.

Every parent should know ...

96

how to lead your
child to Jesus.

97

that moral and ethical
values are best learnt
through the example
of a child's parents.

98

that you should constantly
thank your child's catechists.

99

that God understands the
pain of a suffering child.

100

that prayer is a binding
factor in the life of a family.

101

that a family who practises
their religion together
can withstand any storm.

102

that a child of God-fearing
parents will never be poor.

103

that if the children fall asleep
during public worship,
the time has come to look
for another congregation.

104

that Jesus said, "Let the little
children come to me, and
forbid them not, for of such is the
kingdom of heaven" (cf. Mt. 19:14).

105

how to be an example
of spiritual maturity.

106

how to pray with your children.

107

how to explain basic Christian truths in a language that children can understand.

108

that Jesus Christ said, "Verily I say unto you, Whosoever shall not receive the kingdom of God as a little child, he shall not enter therein" (Mk. 10:15).

<u>10·9</u>

that the more complicated
life becomes, the more simple the
truths that are applied should be.

<u>110</u>

a few action stories from the Bible.

DISCIPLINE (111-147)

*Discipline originates from the same word base
as "disciple," which means follower. Our children should be able to follow in our footsteps
with confidence because they are our dis-
ciples. In this way they can learn to live a dis-
ciplined life. Loving guidance and interven-
tion with our children lie at the root of the discipline that we impress upon them.*

111

that discipline and corporal
punishment are not the same thing.

112

that children don't have an answer
to the question: "How many
times must I tell you this again?"

113

when to say: "That is enough!"

114

how to help your child to
understand the consequences
of his actions and behaviour.

115

that rules will be
disregarded every now and then.

116

how to react when
rules are disregarded.

117

how to provide freedom
and still maintain respect.

118

how to let children feel that
they are a part of family decisions.

Every parent should know ...

119

that children are not
miniature grown-ups.

120

that "It wasn't me!" actually
means, "I'm scared, I've made a
mistake, but I don't want to admit it."

121

The rod and reproof give
wisdom: but a child left
to himself bringeth his
mother to shame (Prov. 29:15).

122

that too much control stifles
the development of a healthy
decision making process.

123

that decisions about
discipline in the house
is seldom democratic.

124

that there are always
exceptions to the rule.

Every parent should know ...

125

that intimidation and
threats don't offer
long-term solutions.

126

how to establish boundaries and to
explain why they are necessary.

127

that the sentence "Do
as I say and not as I
do," has no credibility
in the eyes of a child.

Every parent should know ...

<u>128</u>

that threats seldom
convince a child.

<u>129</u>

how to react when your
child wants to side-
step or ignore a challenge.

<u>130</u>

not to ... provoke ... your
children to wrath: but bring
them up in the nurture and
admonition of the Lord (Eph. 6:4).

<u>131</u>

how to cultivate an attitude
of mercy by sometimes expecting
failure and to allow it as well.

<u>132</u>

foolishness is bound in the
heart of a child; but the
rod of correction shall drive
it far from him (Prov. 22:15).

<u>133</u>

that every justified punishment is more
effective than ten lectures or threats.

<u>134</u>

that a child who mis-
behaves is very often
a discouraged child.

<u>135</u>

that you should find fault
with what your child has
done and not with who he is.

<u>136</u>

what the theology
of mercy means.

137

when to substitute a
lecture with calm questioning.

138

he that spareth his rod hateth
his son: but he that loveth him
chasteneth him betimes (Prov. 13:24).

139

how to discipline
without harming character.

140

that children who become
grown-ups are usually thankful
for the discipline of their youth.

141

a good spiritual leader is
a parent who exercises his
authority over his children in
a dignified way (cf. 1 Tim. 4:4).

142

how to spell "immediately."

143

when to give your children some space.

144

how to determine whether
your discipline is just,
excessive or indulgent.

145

that things are different
today than when the parents
of today were children.

146

never to punish a child twice
for the same transgression.

147

that punishment and
reproof in public are more
destructive than constructive.

SCHOOL AND
ACHIEVEMENTS (148-171)

*A large part of our children's development years
are spent in school. It is the parent's duty to
take part in the planning of his child's school
career and also to be part of it. Achievement
must be seen as a gift from God and not as the
result of pressure from a parent.*

148

that every minute of your child's life
does not have to be crammed with
classes, lessons and organised sport.

149

that a child's attitude
towards his work is much
more important than his skill.

150

that academic success in
primary school, or even in
high school, is not a guarantee
of success at college or university.

151

that knowledge is much more
important than examination marks.

152

when to emphasise the positive.

153

how to accept less than
perfect examination results.

154

how to use an encyclopaedia
and a dictionary.

155

that parents should know
the map of the world.

156

how to identify a good school.

157

the name of the school nurse.

158

that raising a child with
character is more important
than a mantelpiece full of trophies.

159

how to cultivate attainable
expectations in your child.

160

you ought to praise and encourage
your child profusely and generously.

161

what contribution you should
make to your child's classroom.

162

that their best is all
your children can do.

163

how to encourage
children to participate.

164

to treasure and keep all sports
awards, art works and report cards.

165

you ought to have a thorough
awareness of what your child excels at.

166

never to place pressure on
your child to perform well.

167

that growth goes hand
in hand with failure.

168

that you should determine
a specific time for your children
to do their homework.

169

that every child has a gift.

170

who your child's teachers are.

<u>171</u>

that when children ask for
help with their homework,
they are looking for answers
and not for a thirty minute lecture
on the origin of the subject.

COMMUNICATION (172-188)

*We should make time to talk to our children.
Communication does not merely involve talk-
ing, but also listening. There must be an open
channel between the hearts of family members so that thoughts can flow freely in order
to create mutual understanding and support.*

<u>172</u>

how to talk to children about
their experiences of the past day.

173

that they should consider
their words carefully. The
spoken word can never be erased.

174

how to calm down before reacting.

175

that writing notes and letters
to your children lays the
foundation for communication.

176

how to ask "How do you
feel about ... ?" questions.

~ ☾☾ ~

177

that you should teach
your children how to
answer the telephone.

178

how to listen to
your child attentively.

179

how to talk frankly
and honestly to your
child about sexuality.

180

that communication during
meals improves when the
phone is taken off the hook
and the television is switched off.

181

how to whisper.

182

how to talk frankly
about the danger of drugs.

183

that children find the
long conversations of
grown-ups utterly boring.

~ 🌞 ~

184

to phone your children
when they are away from home.

185

that the average father spends less
than five minutes a day educating
and communicating with his child.

186

when to bite your
tongue and keep quiet.

187

how to bargain.

<u>188</u>

that trips in the car are
an opportunity for
family members to bond.

VACATION, SPORT
AND LEISURE (189-225)

*A balanced family life includes regular and
constructive leisure. The interest of a parent
is essential for a child's participation in sport.
A family vacation is no substitute for development within the family.*

<u>189</u>

that you should read to
your children ... and
they should learn to read.

190

how to make a kite
... and make it fly!

191

that one shouldn't play
on the railway tracks.

192

what the names of the
seven dwarfs in Snow-White are.

193

that buying at least one
Disney video is an investment.

<u>194</u>

how to calculate batting averages.

<u>195</u>

how to make a map of
the country with dough.

<u>196</u>

when it is story time at the local library.

<u>197</u>

five activities the family
can enjoy together.

198

how to organise a birthday party
... and ensure that it runs smoothly.

199

a few good games
to play in the car for
those long journeys.

200

about at least one
restaurant in the vicinity
that enjoys catering for children.

201

you ought to play indoor
games with your
children on rainy days.

202

how to bake mud
pies with your children.

203

what the names of
the top ten videos are.

204

that it is important to often go
out with your children.

205

how to identify with your
children's music and
not be negative about it.

206

how to utilise summer
days to the maximum.

207

how to teach your
children the true meaning
of sportsmanship.

208

how important it is to
do family things together.

209

you ought to go and see a
movie at the drive-in theatre.

210

which vacation programmes
are offered by the school.

211

how to organise a treasure hunt.

212

that young children enjoy
camping with their parents.

213

how to build a sand
castle on the beach.

214

when the children's
different sports
seasons start.

215

when to take a brief,
unexpected holiday.

216

of an animal
shelter close to you.

217

a few of the top ten music
hits the teenagers like.

218

how to pick good
books for your children.

219

that family vacations create
memories that last a lifetime.

220

that your children will not remember
whether the cake was home-baked
or bought, but that they will
remember that they had a party.

<u>221</u>

how to encourage your
children to exercise.

<u>222</u>

that your children are proud
to bring their friends home.

<u>223</u>

how to throw a frisbee.

<u>224</u>

that children need healthy exercise.

225

how to play your
children's favourite games.

MONEY AND MATERIAL POSSESSIONS (226-242)

A child must learn at an early age how to work with money and possessions. One should, however, still guard against the cult of money worship.

226

that when parents
are obsessed with
buying, the children will
follow in their footsteps.

<u>227</u>

you ought to teach
your child how to make
use of a money box.

<u>228</u>

that children who have
everything, appreciate nothing.

<u>229</u>

how to teach your children
to make their own cards
for Christmas and birthdays.

230

that children cost
a lot of money.

231

where to buy clothes
at lower prices.

232

that the more toys you
give children to dispel
boredom, the more they
will expect to receive.

Every parent should know ...

<u>233</u>

to write your children's
names on their clothes
before they go on a camp.

<u>234</u>

that if a child is not happy at heart,
gifts are not going to do any good.

<u>235</u>

that a child can never
receive enough pocket money.

~ 83 ~

236.

that children must learn
not to believe all
advertisements automatically.

237

where you can buy sports
equipment for your child at
the lowest possible price.

238

that children need excitement
to look forward to, not
possessions to recall.

239

how to save for
your child's education.

240

that you should help your
children to notice people
who are suffering.

241

that mementoes
become family memories.

242

which restaurants allow
small children to eat for free.

ADOLESCENCE (243-256)

The storm and stress years of the teenager are a trying time for parents and children alike. Adolescence is truly a test for practical Christian parenthood. Only through patience and love do we as parents pass this test. So many of us fail horribly and very few pass cum laude.

243

that teenagers don't
like being seen with
their parents in public.

Every parent should know ...

244

that half the adolescents in
our country are sexually active.

245

what the danger
signals of drug abuse are.

246

that you shouldn't
underestimate suicide threats.

247

that puberty makes
children strange and
parents incomprehensible.

248

that your child's friends most
probably have better parents.

249

that adolescence means love letters,
an interest in the opposite sex and
falling in love at least once a month
... and then breaking up again.

Every parent should know ...

250

that only in heaven
will you finally be rid
of teenage problems.

251

that while there are teenagers
in the house, the parents
never own the phone.

252

where to obtain information
regarding drug dependency.

253

how to talk frankly and
honestly about sexuality.

254

that children now enjoy the
rights of grown-ups long
before their parents did.

255

that God used David to
defeat Goliath
while he was still a teenager.

256

that calf-love is
extremely important to calves.

HUMOUR AND LAUGHTER (257-265)

*A family where healthy humour and constant
laughter is part of every day, is undoubtedly
a happy family. He who hasn't discovered this
gift from God, deprives himself and his family. Healthy Christian humour is like medicine
for the heart and for our relationships.*

257

that a house filled with
laughter, pranks, jokes
and silliness is a happy home.

258

that a bit of humour
is always beneficial.

259

a few bedtime joys
to help your children
fall asleep quickly.

260

how important it is
to be able to laugh.

261

how to perform a few
magic tricks skilfully.

262

how to be outright silly.

263

how to laugh at your
own mistakes and failures.

264

you ought to have at
least three silly family secrets.

2.6.5

why curiosity killed the cat.

MARRIAGE (266-272)

The marriage of a child's parents is an example to the child with regard to the role he will fulfil in his own marriage one day. This places a grave responsibility on the shoulders of every parent, but the reward is endless if the child eventually says: "One day I want a marriage just like my parents'."

2.6.6

that children feel secure when they see that their parents love each other.

<u>267</u>

that the best gift parents
can give their children is
their love for each other.

<u>268</u>

that children feel insecure
when their parents are
fighting with each other.

<u>269</u>

how important it is to
work on your marriage.

270✩

the date of the next marriage
enrichment course
offered by your congregation.

271

that small children find
it almost impossible to
understand divorce.

272

that children want to know
how their parents fell in love.

TELEVISION (273-279)

Parents should teach their children to watch television with discernment. Sometimes one should take a definite stand when it is justified. We cannot monitor everything our children see and hear, but we can (and must) guide them towards the positive.

273

that children watch between 22 and 25 hours of television per week.

274

when to lock the television cabinet.

275

at least five fun activities
to replace watching television.

276

that television is a
source of negative values.

277

that television smothers
a child's creativity, while
reading stimulates it.

Every parent should know ...

278

that more or less twenty
thousand implied sexual
acts are shown on television
every year and that almost
all of them are extramarital.

279

where and how to complain
about bad television programmes.

EMERGENCY SITUATIONS (280-285)
Just like pleasant surprises, emergency situations also pop up in family life. We should be willing and able to handle these situations. We can only do this if we live close to the Lord.

~ 99 ~

280

how to stop the blood while
your child is waiting for stitches.

281

how to apply
artificial respiration.

282

someone who can be
contacted in the
case of an emergency.

283

the telephone number
of your nearest
ambulance service.

284

that all emergency numbers
should be close at hand.

285

what the normal body
temperature is, so that you
will be able to diagnose a fever.

FOOD AND MEALS (286-300)

Parents are not always aware of the importance of food in the life of a family. To teach children to eat "right" is a challenge all parents have to face some time. Scripture also offers a few wise words in this regard.

286:

a special recipe to
make special custard.

287

that one should always have
snacks somewhere in the house.

Every parent should know ...

288

a traditional family recipe
that you can pass on
to the next generation.

289

to always have an extra
place ready at the table
for an unexpected friend.

290

how to make sandwiches
in such a way that
other children envy yours.

~ 103 ~

Every parent should know ...

291

how to pack a picnic basket.

292

that junk food should be the
exception and not the normal diet.

293

that an overloaded fridge can
contain nothing for a child to eat.

294

what your child's
favourite pudding is.

295

that your children's table
manners will indeed improve
before they turn twenty-one.

296

that runaways always return
home again before supper.

297

that a child's appetite
varies from day to day.

298

how to avoid the shelf with
sweets when you are
shopping with the children.

299

how important it is to
enjoy your meals together.

300

that complex carbohydrates
such as pasta and bread
are the most effective source
of energy to get your
children through the day.

GENERAL (301-365)

There are always a number of unexpected things that make family life exciting and interesting. You should also experience these adventures in view of the Bible.

301

each child is a unique,
once-off creation of God.

302

normal children hate taking
a bath, brushing their teeth
and changing their underwear.

303

never to leave children under
the age of ten at home alone.

304

that children just love
exciting tales from the
days when you were growing up.

305

how to be a dignified loser.

306

that photographs are
extremely precious.

307

that there is always a
difficult way of doing everything.

308

that the logic of a child
is not always rational.

309

that you can be irresponsible
with your income, but
not with your children.

310

how to create
positive memories.

311

how to change
a weakness into
a strength.

312

that children learn by
watching their parents.

Every parent should know ...

313

a recipe for cheering
up any difficult moment.

314

you ought to attach
your children's master-
pieces to the fridge door.

315

that mud can easily
be rinsed out.

316

that a happy family
is a little piece of
heaven here on earth.

317

that a firearm lying around
somewhere in the house will
most probably be used as a toy.

318

that small hands cannot
work as skilfully as big ones.

319

that children are far
sharper than they seem.

320

that the reasoning of a
child is not always logical.

321

of something that is
special about your child.

322

how to help your children
to accept responsibility
for their own actions.

323

that very few parents on their
death bed wish that they had
spent more time on their work.

324

your own weaknesses
and shortcomings.

325

not to make mountains
out of molehills.

326

that children very seldom
believe, understand or
follow the principles their
parents are passionate about.

327

that quality time and quantity
time are equally important.

328

how to create a master-
piece from leftovers.

329

that safety belts save lives.

330

to display your child's
latest piece of art
somewhere in the house.

331

how to drive dragons and
giants out from under the bed.

332

you ought to teach your
child what fingerprints are.

333

that the back pocket of
a child's trousers can
also contain chewing
gum, sweets and marbles.

334

that the tooth fairy does exist
up to the age of eight – after
which the children just
play along for the money.

335

that every birthday should be a
unique celebration and memory.

336.

that you regularly ought to
tell at least one boastful
story from your youth.

337

that it should be safe
to put a "Don't disturb"
sign on your door.

338

that children
hate sitting still.

339

that children don't
have price tags.

340

that children don't believe
that their parents walked
through kilometres of
snow to get to school.

341

that children seek
popularity, but
that their parents
are seldom popular.

342

that Murphy's law
claims: "If something
can go wrong, it will."

343

to expect the unexpected.

344

that children desire
importance, just as
parents desire wealth.

<u>345</u>

when to buy your
child earphones.

<u>346</u>

that children prefer working
in the neighbour's house.

<u>347</u>

that you should teach your
child how to ask questions.

<u>348</u>

how much it means
to children when their
parents attend their functions.

<u>349</u>

that parents on television
are always portrayed as being
old-fashioned and reactionary.

<u>350</u>

that a child's perception
always seems like
the truth to him.

351

how to notice progress.

352

that children notice their
parents' drinking habits.

353

that children are more
creative when they are bored.

354

which things capture their
children's attention.

Every parent should know ...

355

why it is so beneficial
to create a family life.

356

how to get rid of
tomato sauce stains.

357

that an ordinary cold
isn't the result of
walking barefoot.

358

that children are gifts
from God (cf. Ps. 127:3).

359

how to apply sunscreen.

360

that change can be enjoyed.

361

how to explain where
pets go after they have died.

362

that the best way of ending a doctor's
appointment is with an ice-cream.

Every parent should know ...

363

that it is all right to
sometimes make a mess.

364

how to give a child medicine
without him complaining.

365

to keep an emergency gift
hidden somwhere in a cupboard
for that unexpected celebration.